BULLETPOINTS

MYTHS & LEGENDS
EPIC HEROES

Vic Parker

Miles Kelly
PUBLISHING

First published by Miles Kelly Publishing Ltd
Bardfield Centre, Great Bardfield, Essex, CM7 4SL

Copyright © 2004 Miles Kelly Publishing
Some material in this book first appeared in *1000 Things You Should Know*

2 4 6 8 10 9 7 5 3 1

Editor: Kate Miles

Art Director: Debbie Meekcoms

Design Assistant: Tom Slemmings

Picture Research: Liberty Newton

Production: Estela Boulton

British Library Cataloguing-in-Publication Data
A catalogue record for this book is available from the British Library

ISBN 1-84236-401-4

Printed in China

www.mileskelly.net
info@mileskelly.net

The publishers would like to thank the following artists whose work appears in this book:
Peter Dennis, Nicholas Forder, Sally Holmes, Richard Hook, John James, Barry Jones, Chris Odgers,
Terry Riley, Susan Scott, Gwen Tourret, Rudi Vizi, Steve Weston

The publishers would also like to thank the following photographic sources:
Page 7 The Art Archive/Archaeological Museum Aleppo Syria/Dagli Orti;
25 New Line Productions/Pictorial Press; 37 Margaret Courtney-Clarke/Corbis

All other photographs from MKP Archives: Corel, Corbis, Hemera, PHOTODISC

Contents

The oral tradition

- **Myths and legends existed** in civilizations all over the world for thousands of years before writing was developed. They were told as entertainment by professional poets specially trained to remember the long works and perform them out loud. This is called the oral tradition of literature.

- **An epic is an adventure story** in the form of a long poem, which follows the brave deeds of a human hero as he struggles against magical dangers.

- **The heroes of many epics** are often born into royalty and brought up away from their parents.

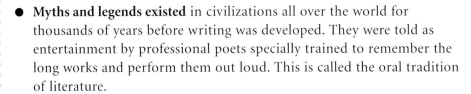

▼ *One of the enduring Greek stories is of Daedalus, whose son Icarus flew too close to the sun, melting the wax on the wings that had been crafted for him to escape from King Minos.*

- **Many epic heroes** possess superhuman powers and are helped by gods or spirits.

- **Most epic heroes** possess at least one magical weapon or object with magic powers.

- **Epic poetry provided** early peoples with standards and goals for how to live a good life.

▶ *The crews of these Ancient Greek triremes sailed off to do battle with ships and lands taking with them their stories of legends and myths.*

- **The most famous epics** are the Greek poems *The Iliad* and *The Odyssey*. Some historians think these were written by a blind man called Homer around 750BC. Others think they were composed gradually in the oral tradition by a series of poets.

- **Archaeologists have found** written fragments of *The Iliad* and *The Odyssey* dating from the fourth century BC. However, the oldest complete manuscripts are dated from the tenth century AD.

- **Medieval poets were called bards** or troubadors. They often chanted their tales to music.

> **FASCINATING FACT**
> The name for traditional storytellers in some parts of Africa was griots.

Gilgamesh

- **This epic poem is from Sumeria** – one of the earliest civilizations to have city states, laws and irrigation.

- **Gilgamesh was a real king** of the Sumerian city Uruk, around 2700–2500BC.

- **In the poem, King Gilgamesh** is a man of mighty strength who is loved dearly by the gods.

- **When the nobles of Uruk** complain to the gods that King Gilgamesh is a tyrant, the Mother Goddess makes a hero called Enkidu to challenge him. Gilgamesh meets his match in Enkidu, and the two become firm friends.

- **When Enkidu dies**, Gilgamesh begins to fear his own death. He embarks on a quest to find out how to become immortal.

- **Gilgamesh does not win eternal life**, but is rewarded with a plant which will keep him young and strong for the rest of his days. When a watersnake steals it from him, he nearly despairs.

- **Gilgamesh finally realizes** that the only type of immortality humans can achieve is fame through performing great deeds and building lasting monuments.

- **The poem was discovered in 1845**, when archaeologists were excavating at the ancient city of Nineveh.

- **Experts think that** *Gilgamesh* was first written down on clay tablets in an ancient language called cuneiform. It is the earliest recorded major work of literature.

- **Fragments of** *Gilgamesh* have been found by archaeologists in ancient sites throughout many countries of the Middle East.

▲ *This ancient Sumerian stone relief shows the hero Gilgamesh as the central figure.*

Heracles's labours

- **Heracles was Zeus's son** by a mortal woman. Zeus's divine wife, Hera, was so jealous that she would only allow Zeus to make Heracles immortal if Heracles could complete a series of impossible tasks.

- **Unlike other Greek heroes**, Heracles does not set out seeking fame, fortune and immortality. He only performs the labours because it is commanded by the gods.

- **Two labours involved killing** terrifying beasts: the man-eating Nemean lion and a nine-headed, poisonous swamp monster called the Hydra.

- **Four labours involved** capturing magical creatures alive: the golden deer sacred to the goddess Artemis, the vicious Erymanthian boar, a ferocious bull belonging to the god Poseidon, and some flesh-eating horses.

- **One labour was to get rid** of a flock of birds who shot their feathers like arrows at people.

▲ *An ancient Greek statue of the formidable father god, Zeus.*

- **Two labours involved stealing** precious objects: the belt of the fearsome Amazon queen, Hippolyte, and a herd of cattle belonging to the giant, Geryon.

- **A humiliating labour was** to clean out the biggest, dirtiest stables in the world.

- **The final labours required** journeying to the ends of the Earth to fetch some golden apples and venturing into the Underworld to bring back the three-headed guard dog, Cerberus.

- **After many further adventures**, Heracles was finally poisoned. As he lay dying, Zeus took him up to Mount Olympus, at last to join the gods as an immortal.

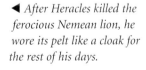

- **In ancient times**, Heracles was the most popular Greek hero. Today, there are TV shows, films and cartoons all based on the myth.

◄ *After Heracles killed the ferocious Nemean lion, he wore its pelt like a cloak for the rest of his days.*

9

Jason & the Argonauts

- **According to Ancient Greek** myth, Jason was a prince of Iolcus who was exiled from his home as a child when his uncle seized the throne.

- **A wise centaur called Chiron** brought up Jason with other abandoned future heroes, including the mighty warriors Achilles and Aeneas.

- **It was the centaur**, Chiron, who gave Jason his name. It means 'healer'.

- **Jason returned** to Iolchus to claim his throne. His uncle agreed to give up the throne if Jason travelled to the ends of the earth and brought back a magical Golden Fleece.

- **Jason built a huge ship** for the voyage, called the *Argo*. The goddess Athene gave a magic bough for the prow, which was able to speak words of advice.

- **The greatest heroes** in Greek mythology, including Heracles, volunteered to help Jason in his task. They became known as the Argonauts.

- **Jason and the Argonauts** faced peril after peril on their sea voyage. Many of these were reworked later into the epic poem, *The Odyssey*.

- **A beautiful witch-girl** called Medea fell in love with Jason. She used her magic to help Jason win the Golden Fleece from its owner and escape. It belonged to the king of Colchis – her own father.

- **The name Medea** means 'cunning'.

- **Jason later left Medea**, breaking an oath to the gods. This brought trouble upon him. Some said that Medea murdered him in revenge. Others believed that he died an old beggar man.

▲ *One hazard*
encountered by Jason and the
Argonauts on their voyage was the
Symplegades. These were rocks which clashed
together, crushing ships passing between them.

Theseus's adventures

- **There are many myths** about a hero called Theseus who became king of Attica in Greece. Historians have proved that a real King Theseus did once exist.

- **According to legends**, Theseus was the secret son of a king called Aegeus. Theseus was brought up away from Attica, to keep him safe from enemies who wanted the throne for themselves.

- **As a young man**, Theseus travelled to Attica to claim his birthright. He chose a long route through many dangers, because he wanted to prove himself on the way.

- **Theseus once took** a mighty bronze-plated club from a thug who tried to kill him. He used the weapon for the rest of his life.

- **Theseus liked to punish criminals** by their own evil methods. One villain liked to tie people between two bent young trees which sprang back and ripped them apart. Thanks to Theseus, he got a dose of his own medicine.

- **When Theseus reached Attica**, his father's new wife tried to poison him. Luckily King Aegeus recognized his son just in time.

◄ *Myth says that the Minotaur was created when the god Poseidon cruelly caused King Minos's wife to fall in love with a magnificent bull. Their affair resulted in a child with a human body and a bull's head.*

▲ *A perfect example of Doric architecture, a temple to the goddess of Athens, Athene, was built in 447BC. Today it is called the Parthenon.*

- **Each year, Aegeus** had to send young people as a human sacrifice to King Minos of Crete. Brave Thesesus volunteered to go. He was thrown into a maze called the Labyrinth to be eaten by a ferocious bull-headed man, the Minotaur. Instead, Theseus slew the monster.

- **King Minos's daughter**, Ariadne, fell in love with Theseus and helped him to escape from the Labyrinth.

- **Archaeologists have found** that the ancient royal palace of Crete was laid out rather like a maze, and that a dangerous sport a bit like bull-fighting was very popular. The myth of the Minotaur might have arisen from stories about them.

- **Historians credit Theseus** with building Athens as an important Greek centre of power. Today it is the capital of the country.

The Trojan War

- *The Iliad* **is an epic poem** which tells of events at the end of a ten-year war between the Ancient Greeks and the Trojans.

- **The Trojan War** began when a Trojan nobleman called Paris kidnapped Helen, Queen of Sparta. Her father asked the Greeks to help win her back.

- **When *The Iliad* was composed**, no written records about the Trojan War existed. The story comes from information passed down by word of mouth for hundreds of years.

- **The city of Troy definitely existed**, as archaeologists have discovered its remains. The city burned in 1184BC.

- **The principal characters** in *The Iliad* are the courageous noblemen of both sides. They aim to win fame by fighting honourably and dying a glorious warrior's death.

◀ *The Trojan War ended when Greek warriors secretly entered the city of Troy by hiding inside a huge wooden horse.*

- **The greatest Greek warrior** is Achilles. When he argues with the Greek commander, Agamemnon, and withdraws from battle, the Greek army suffers terribly.

- **The greatest Trojan warrior** is Paris's brother, Hector.

- **Goddesses and gods play a major** role in *The Iliad*. They support different sides, just as if they were football teams, giving their human favourites advice and help.

- *The Iliad* **is the earliest** written work from Ancient Greece.

- **The Greeks eventually won** the Trojan War. The hero Odysseus had the idea of building a huge wooden horse, inside which many Greek warriors hid. The Greeks left it outside the gates of Troy and the Trojans took it inside the city, thinking it was a gift. At night, the Greek warriors scrambled out and destroyed the city.

▲ *This painting on an ancient Greek vase shows the warrior Achilles. He was protected by divine armour – except for a small spot on his heel, which is where he finally received his death wound.*

Odysseus & The Odyssey

- **The Odyssey is an adventure** story which follows the Greek hero, Odysseus, after the Trojan War, on his long and difficult sea voyage home.

- **Odysseus and his men** have to face many magical dangers on their journey, including monsters and giants.

- **On one occasion**, some of Odysseus's sailors eat lotus fruit, which makes them forget all about returning to their families and homes.

- **Odysseus has to sail safely** past the Sirens. These are half-woman, half-bird creatures who live on a craggy seashore. They sing a magical song that lures sailors to steer their ships onto the rocks to their deaths.

- **The goddess of war**, Athena, acts as Odysseus's patron, giving him special help and guidance.

- **The sea god Poseidon** hates Odysseus and seeks to shipwreck him.

- **By the time Odysseus finally** reaches his palace in Ithaca, he has been away for 20 years. Disguised as a beggar, only his faithful old dog recognizes him.

▲ One Greek legend says that the Sirens were so furious when Odysseus escaped their clutches that they drowned themselves .

> ...FASCINATING FACT...
> Unlike its companion poem, *The Iliad*,
> *The Odyssey* has a happy ending.

- **Once home, Odysseus's troubles** are not over. Powerful suitors are pressurizing his faithful wife, Penelope, for her hand in marriage, so they can seize Odysseus's crown.

- **Women often hold positions** of great power in the poem. For instance, Circe is a very powerful sorceress who turns some of Odysseus's sailors into pigs. The goddess Calypso keeps Odysseus captive on her island for seven years.

▶ *After 20 years at war, Odysseus returns to his kingdom disguised as a beggar. He is greeted by his old dog, who then dies content.*

The Aeneid

- *The Aeneid* **is an epic poem which follows** the adventures of a Trojan prince, Aeneas, after the end of the Trojan War.

- *The Aeneid* **was not composed** in the oral tradition. The Roman author, Virgil, wrote it down in Latin.

- **Virgil was the well-educated son** of a farmer. The Roman Emperor, Augustus Caesar, recognized his writing talent and became his patron (supported him with money).

- **Virgil based the legends** in his poem and its structure on the epics *The Iliad* and *The Odyssey*.

- **In *The Iliad*, Aeneas fights** many times against the Greeks, but is always saved by the gods because he has another destiny.

- **It was popular in the sixth century** BC to picture part of the legend of Aeneas on vases – how Aeneas carried his father to safety out of the smoking ruins of Troy.

- **Virgil designed *The Aeneid*** to give Augustus and the Roman empire a glorious history. It explains that the gods themselves instructed Aeneas to travel to Italy, to be the ancestor of a great race – the Romans. It shows how Augustus Caesar was directly descended from the mighty hero.

- **In *The Aeneid*, Aeneas falls in love** with Queen Dido of Carthage and then abandons her, sailing for Italy. Virgil probably made up this myth to explain the hatred that existed between Rome and Carthage in the third century BC.

- **Virgil began *The Aeneid*** in 29BC and worked on it for the last ten years of his life. As he lay dying of a fever, he asked for the poem to be burnt. However, Augustus Caesar overruled his wishes.

● **A great Italian poet** called Dante Alighieri (1265–1321) used Virgil's style and the legends of *The Aeneid* as the basis for his own poem, the *Divine Comedy*.

▶ *According to one ancient source, the poet Virgil was tall and dark with the appearance of a countryman.*

Romulus & Remus

- **The story of Romulus and Remus** tells how twin boys grew up to build the foundations of the mighty city of Rome.

- **Versions of the myth were written** by many of the greatest Roman writers, such as Livy, Plutarch and Virgil.

- **According to the legend**, Romulus and Remus were descendants of the hero Aeneas. They were the sons of a princess and the war god, Mars.

- **As babies, the twin boys** were cast out by their evil great-uncle, who had stolen the king's crown from their grandfather. They survived because a she-wolf found them and let them drink her milk. A bird also fed them by placing crumbs in their mouths.

▶ *The Roman legend of Romulus and Remus may have been the inspiration for the Tarzan story. In both cases, abandoned infants were brought up by animals.*

- **When the twins grew** up they overthrew their wicked uncle, restoring their father to his rightful throne.

- **The twins built a new city** on the spot where they had been rescued by the she-wolf. However, they quarrelled about who should be ruler, and Romulus killed Remus.

- **Romulus became king** of the new city and named it Rome, after himself.

- **The new city had too many men** and not enough women. Romulus hatched a plot whereby he held a great celebration and invited neighbouring communities – then captured all their women!

- **Romulus built a strong army**, to defend Rome from attacks by local tribes. He brought about a 40-year period of peace.

- **One day, Romulus was surrounded** by a storm cloud and taken up to heaven, where he became a god.

▶ *You can still see the ruins of the mighty ancient city of Rome in the modern-day Italian capital. The huge round amphitheatre called the Colosseum overshadows the impressive central square, or Forum.*

Beowulf

- **The epic poem** *Beowulf* was written in the Anglo-Saxon language by an unknown English person around AD700–750.

- **The legend focuses on the adventures** of a Viking hero, Beowulf. The action takes place in the south of Sweden and Denmark.

- **Christianity was introduced** to England around AD600. The poem blends traditional elements of Norse myth such as warrior culture and fate with belief in a Christian god.

- **Beowulf risks his own life** to help other people by battling three terrifying monsters: Grendel, Grendel's mother, and a dragon.

- **The monster Grendel** is said to bear 'the mark of Cain'. This is a reference to the Bible story in which Adam's son Cain killed his brother Abel.

- **Beowulf is fatally wounded** when all his chosen warriors desert him through fear – except for his courageous nephew Wiglaf.

- **At the end of the poem**, the dead Beowulf is laid to rest in a huge burial mound. A similarly impressive burial mound, dating around AD650, was discovered at Sutton Hoo in Suffolk in 1939.

- **The oldest manuscript** of *Beowulf* that exists today was made from an original by monks in about AD1000. Many other older copies were destroyed when King Henry VIII ordered monasteries and their libraries to be closed down in the late 1530s.

◄ *This helmet was buried along with many other treasures in a splendid longboat in the seventh century at Sutton Hoo in Suffolk, England. Historians think the treasures belonged to an important Anglo-Saxon king.*

- **The modern-day film** *The Thirteenth Knight*, starring Antonio Banderas, is based on the gripping Beowulf legend.

- **The only remaining copy** is kept in a controlled environment behind glass in the British Museum.

▼ *Beowulf descends to the depths of a murky lake to fight the monster Grendel's ferocious mother.*

Sigurd the Volsung

- **Different versions of the legend** of the warrior hero Sigurd the Volsung exist in Norse, British and German mythologies.

- **The earliest existing written** version appears as part of the Norse epic poem, *Beowulf*, where a storyteller recites the saga as entertainment for some warrior nobles.

- **The most detailed** version of the myth is known as *The Volsunga Saga* (written around AD1300 by an unknown author).

- **The legend is a superb adventure** story about heroic deeds, magic, love, betrayal, jealousy, danger and death.

  - **Volsung is the King of Hunland**, and great-grandson of the Norse father of the gods, Odin.

  - **Volsung's son, Sigmund**, is similarly mighty. In an episode which parallels the legend of the young King Arthur pulling the sword from the stone, Sigmund is the only man who can pull Odin's sword out of an oak tree trunk.

  - **Odin's favourite is Sigmund's son**, the hero Sigurd. Odin helps Sigurd choose a horse that is related to his own magical steed.

◄ *The hero Sigurd and his adventures were the subject of several operas by the nineteenth-century German composer Richard Wagner.*

- **Odin's sword was smashed** when Sigmund died. Sigurd has the fragments recast into a fearsome weapon called Gram.

- **Sigurd's first quest is to find** a hoard of dwarf gold, guarded by a dragon. One of the treasures is a cursed ring. This inspired the modern-day author J R R Tolkien in his *Lord of the Rings* books and also the composer Wagner in his series of operas, *The Ring of the Nibelung.*

▶ *J R R Tolkien's* Lord of the Rings *saga, inspired by the Sigurd legend, has recently been made into three award-winning movies.*

> **FASCINATING FACT**
> The saga contains an early version of the story of *Beauty and the Beast.*

25

King Arthur

◀ *Mont-Saint-Michel is a rocky islet off the coast of northwest France, where legend says King Arthur once slew a giant.*

- **Legends about an extraordinary** British king called Arthur have been popular for over 800 years, yet historians have never been able to prove whether he was a real figure in history.

- **If a real Arthur** did exist, he is likely to have lived much earlier than the medieval times of the legends.

- **Many authors have written** Arthurian legends over the centuries, including: the French medieval poet Chretien de Troyes, the fifteenth-century writer Sir Thomas Malory, and the Victorian poet Lord Tennyson.

- **Arthur's father was said** to be King Uther Pendragon. The name means 'dragon's head'.

▶ *King Arthur was finally killed by his own son. One legend says that his body was buried at the holy site of Glastonbury.*

- **One legend says that Arthur** slew a fearsome giant at Mont-Saint-Michel in France, then conquered the Roman Empire.

- **Many legends focus on the knights** at Arthur's court and the idea of courtly love, in which women are purer beings in God's eyes than men. A lover knight is required to obey the wishes of his lady without question or reward.

- **Arthur's knights went on many** dangerous quests to test their bravery and honour. The most difficult was a search for the Holy Grail – a goblet that caught Jesus's blood as he died on the cross. It was believed to disappear when anyone who had sinned came near it.

- **The Round Table** was first mentioned in legends written by the French medieval poet, Robert Wace, in AD1155.

- **Arthur is finally killed** by his enemy Mordred – who is in fact his own son.

- **Some legends say that King Arthur** was taken to a country of blessed souls called Avalon and will return when Britain falls into greatest danger.

Cuchulain

- **The correct way to pronounce** Cuchulain is 'Cu-hoo-lin'.

- **Cuchulain was a warrior hero** supposed to have lived in Ireland in the first century AD.

- **Stories say that Cuchulain was born** when the king of Ulster's sister was magically swept away by a god called Lug. However, the baby's name was originally Setanta.

- **Setanta was schooled by the greatest heroes** and poets at the king of Ulster's court.

- **As a teenager, Setanta killed single-handed a ferocious dog** belonging to a blacksmith called Culan. This is how he got his nickname, because Cuchulain means 'Hound of Culan'.

- **Cathbad the Druid once prophesied** that any boy who became a warrior that day would become the most famous hero in all Ireland – but would die young. Cuchulain was 15, but decided to arm himself to fulfil the prophecy. He wanted a short, glorious life rather than a longer, more unremarkable one.

- **Cuchulain was a rare thing called a 'berserk warrior'**. This means that he was possessed by a frenzy in battle. Power sparked from his hair, his body hissed with heat, his eyes bulged, his muscles stretched his skin, and blood frothed on his lips.

- **Cuchulain won his wife**, Emer, by defeating the tricks of a cunning chieftain called Forgal the Wily.

- **Cuchulain died in battle.** He had been terribly wounded, but had lashed himself to a standing stone, so he would die on his feet, fighting to the end.

● **Cathbad the Druid's prediction came true**, because in Irish mythology, Cuchulain is indeed considered to be the greatest of all Irish warrior heroes.

▶ *The Celts believed that a goddess of death called Badb often appeared at battlefields in the form of a raven. According to one legend, a raven drank from the wounded Cuchulain's streaming blood as he fought heroically to his death.*

29

Finn McCool

- **The legend of Finn McCool** might be based on a warrior hero who lived in Ireland in the third century AD.

- **Finn's real name was Demna**. 'Finn' was a nickname meaning 'fair haired'.

- **Finn was raised in secret** by a druidess and a wise woman, who taught him god-like powers of strength and speed.

- **Finn was very wise and just**. This is because he once ate a magical fish called the Salmon of Knowledge.

▲ *Legend says that the hero Finn McCool created the rock formation called the Giants' Causeway in Northern Ireland. In fact, it was formed when lava from a volcano cooled and set.*

- **Finn won the position of head** of the Fianna – an elite group of warriors sworn to defend the High King of Ireland. Under his leadership, the Fianna had many daring, magical adventures and rose to the height of their glory.

- **The Fianna possessed** a magic Treasure Bag which contained weapons from the gods, objects with healing powers, and Faery gifts.

- **Finn fell in love with a goddess,** Sava. She bore him a son, Oisin, who became a famous Fianna warrior and a great poet.

- **Finn once had an argument** with a giant in Scotland. They threw rocks across the sea at one another, which created a rock formation today called the Giants' Causeway.

- **Legend says that Finn** and the Fianna lived on the Hill of Allen in present-day County Kildare.

▲ *This Celtic cross shows Finn McCool with his thumb in his mouth. He is touching his magical 'tooth of knowledge', which had an extraordinary power telling him whatever he wanted to know.*

31

Kotan Utunnai

- **The epic poem *Kotan Utunnai*** belongs to a race of people from the Stone Age called the Ainu.

- **The Ainu lived on** remote Japanese islands, untouched by the outside world for hundreds of years, until other Japanese people made contact in around AD1670.

- **The Ainu were hunter-gatherers** who had no agricultural systems, no metalworking skills and no system of writing.

- **The epic *Kotan Utunnai*** was first written down by an English missionary in the 1880s.

- ***Kotan Utunnai*** is one of several Ainu epic poems which focus on wars with a people called the Okhotsk from the tenth to the sixteenth centuries.

- **Like many epic heroes,** the hero of *Kotan Utunnai* puts family loyalty above his own desires. This means he has to seek revenge for the murder of his parents.

- **In the myth, the world** of humans is strangely mixed up with the magical world of gods, spirits and demons. From time to time humans hear the sound of gods fighting like a low rumbling across the land.

- **Many human epic heroes** have god-like qualities, but the hero of *Kotan Utunnai* is so god-like that even the gods themselves sometimes find it hard to believe he is human!

- **Unlike many other epics,** there are several powerful female characters in *Kotan Utunnai*. Women have great fighting skill and are considered equal in importance with men.

- **The epic demonstrates** the Ainu belief that when you die, if you have led a good life, you will be reborn. However, if you were a wrong-doer, you will remain dead.

▶ *This is an Attush coat worn by the earliest people in Japan, the Ainu. The patterns around all the openings of the coat are designed to stop evil spirits from entering.*

The Ramayana

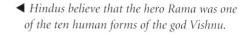

◄ *Hindus believe that the hero Rama was one of the ten human forms of the god Vishnu.*

● **The Indian epic poem** the *Ramayana* focuses on the battle between the forces of good and evil in the universe.

● **Historians believe that it was** largely composed between 200BC and AD200. The poet is believed to be called Valmiki, although hardly anything is known about him.

● **Like the Greek epic *The Iliad*,** the *Ramayana* involves the rescue of a stolen queen (called Sita).

● **Like the Greek epic *The Odyssey*,** the *Ramayana* follows a hero (Prince Rama) on a long and difficult journey.

● **Prince Rama's enemy** is the mighty demon, Ravana. He can work powerful magic, but is not immortal and can be killed.

● **The demon Ravana's followers** are known as Rakshasas. They can shape-shift and disguise themselves so they do not appear evil. This way, they can tempt good people to do the wrong thing.

- **The poem** demonstrates that it is important to respect animals. Rama needs the help of the hero Hanuman and his army of monkeys to rescue Sita.

- **The story says** that Rama and Sita are earthly forms of the great god Vishnu and his wife, Lakshmi.

- **Hindus see the** *Ramayana* as a book of religious teaching because Rama and Sita are models of good behaviour.

- **The legend ends** when Rama has ruled as king for 10,000 years and is taken up to heaven with his brothers.

▶ *The monkey god Hanuman was the son of the wind and a great hero who helped Prince Rama.*

Gassire's Lute

- **An African tribe called the Soninke** have an epic poem called *Gassire's Lute*. It was composed between AD300 and AD1100 as part of a group of songs called the *Dausi*.

- **Most other songs in the *Dausi*** have been forgotten.

- ***Gassire's Lute* is a tale** about the ancestors of the Soninke, a tribe of warrior horsemen called the Fasa.

- **The Fasa lived around** 500BC in a fertile area of Africa bordered by the Sahara Desert, Senegal, Sudan and the river Nile.

- **The hero of the legend**, Gassire, is a Fasa prince who longs for his father to die so he can become a famous king.

- **The heroes of other epic poems** usually put their lives at risk trying to help other people. This epic is strikingly different, because the hero puts his own desires in front of everything else.

- **Gassire realizes that all things die**, and that the only way to win lasting fame is to be remembered as a hero in battle songs.

▲ *A musician plays a lute by plucking its strings, similar to playing the guitar.*

- **Gassire has a lute made,** so he can sing of his own adventures. However, the lute will only play once it has been soaked with blood in battle.

- **Gassire leads his eight sons** and followers into war against an enemy tribe. It is only when all but one of Gassire's sons have been killed that his lute finally sings.

- **Gassire grieves for the dead**, but is filled with joy now he has a great battle song to bring him fame.

◄ *The Fasa ancestors of this Soninke woman were like medieval knights. They fought on horseback with spears and swords, not just in battle but also for sport.*

Mwindo

- **The epic of *Mwindo*** belongs to the Nyanga tribe of Zaire, in Africa.

- **The poem was first written down** in 1956, when the Nyanga tribe still lived by hunting, gathering and growing their food.

- **The poem was performed** as a ritual over 12 days, to give protection from sickness and death.

- **The legend begins** when Chief Shemwindo forbids his wives to bear him any male children. Despite this, a little boy is finally born – Mwindo, which means 'first-born male'.

▲ *Master Lightning is the hero Mwindo's guardian and helper in his adventures.*

- **Shemwindo tries to kill** his son by burying him alive, then by drowning him. Baby Mwindo has superhuman powers which help him escape.

- **Mwindo overcomes his enemies** with the help of friends who include Hedgehog, Spider and Lightning.

- **Mwindo holds a magic sceptre** that he uses to perform powerful spells, such as bringing the dead back to life. He also has a magical bag of good fortune.

- **Mwindo is an example** of good behaviour. He forgives his father and makes peace. In turn, his father makes amends by sharing half of his kingdom with his son.

- **When Mwindo kills** a dragon, Lightning teaches him the lesson that humans are just a part of the universe, not the most powerful thing in it.

- **The main message of the myth** is that all forms of life should have respect for each other: the gods and creation, humans and animals, men and women, the young and the old, the healthy and the sick.

▶ *Storytelling has been a traditional method of keeping myths and legends alive in all cultures.*

Index